Learn Guitar Fast!

Music Theory

Reading Music, Scales, Modes, Chords

Tony Skinner

Produced and created by
FLAME TREE PUBLISHING
Crabtree Hall, Crabtree Lane
Fulham, London, SW6 6TY
United Kingdom
www.flametreepublishing.com
First Published 2004

Publisher and Creative Director: Nick Wells
Editorial: Julia Rolf, Polly Willis
Designer: Jake

Special thanks to Alan Brown at Take Note Publishing for additional diagrams and notation

07 06 05

10 9 8 7 6 5 4 3 2

Flame Tree Publishing is part of the Foundry Creative Media Company Limited

© 2004 Flame Tree Publishing

ISBN 1 84451 133 2

All photographs © Foundry Arts except Live Photography 2, 3 (t 1), 32, London Features International 3 (t 3, b 1), 33, 35, 37 Topham Picturepoint 1, 3 (b 3)

Introduction

Some of the world's greatest guitarists cannot read musical notation – it is not essential if you know your chords and can use TAB – but being able to read music can be an extremely useful skill, especially if you are teaching yourself or if you spend a lot of time playing new music at sessions or jams. For beginners, a sheet of lines, black blobs and unfamiliar symbols can be rather daunting to say the least, but with the help of this no-nonsense guide you will soon find yourself sailing through pieces without even thinking about how they are written.

This book is divided into three sections; the first guides you through the stages of learning to read musical notation, from the basic level of key signatures and clefs, through the uses of notes and rhythms, to the more complex issues of harmony and dynamics. With clear explanations, accompanied by plenty of diagrams and examples, you will soon find yourself progressing onto the more advanced performance material, such as ornamentation and accents.

The second part concentrates on ways in which you can employ your new musical knowledge. Being able to transpose, recognise and reproduce melodies and chords can be very handy if you play in a band. There is also information on how to improve your improvisation skills – invaluable for lead guitarists or for those who play in regular jam sessions.

The third section details the types of scale used in a wide range of different musical styles, from the commonly used major and minor scales to some of the more obscure varieties found in jazz and folk music. Knowing your scales can help with improvising, as well as when writing your own compositions. Notations and fretboxes are provided for all the scales, enabling you to experiment with the various sounds and moods they create.

Contents

The Basics

Reading Music

Although notation for electric and acoustic guitarists is often written in TAB, this has the limitation of not including the rhythmic values, so knowing the sound of the music or listening to an accompanying audio version becomes necessary. However, treble clef notation does not have this limitation, making the ability to read music a useful asset – particularly if you intend to pursue guitar playing to a professional level, or are interested in classical guitar (where TAB is far less frequently used).

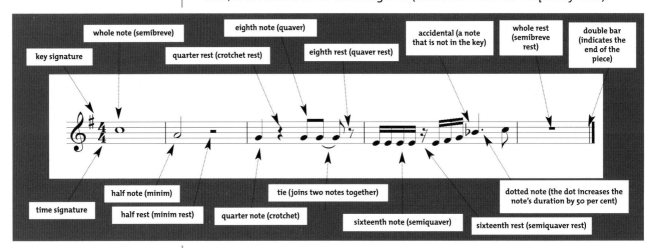

Learning To Sight-Read Music

The first requirement is to look ahead in the score. Looking at a note only as you are about to play it will result, sooner or later, in a problem. By looking ahead you will be prepared for anything difficult. The ideal place to get ahead is before you start: try to memorise the first bar, or more if you can. Then if you can keep looking ahead as you play, you'll always have a breathing space. Once you start playing the piece it is important to keep your eyes on the music. Avoid the temptation to look at the guitar fingerboard, as this may cause you to lose your place in the music. Just look at how a good touch-typist operates: by never looking at the keyboard.

Here are a few other essentials for reliable sight-reading:

- Look at the key signature and the time signature before you start: forgetting either of these will cause errors.

- Once you know the key of the piece, practice the key scale, then use this scale fingering when you play the piece. As you can rely on the scale you won't need to keep looking at the fingerboard to find where to put your fingers.
- Scan through the piece before you play it, trying to identify any awkward rhythms or combinations of notes. If there's time, take the difficult passages aside and practise them separately.
- Avoid the temptation to play the piece too fast, especially if the first few bars look easy. Base your tempo on the speed at which you can perform the most difficult bar.
- Whatever happens, do not stop. All musicians make errors when reading music; it is just that the best ones do not let the audience know. The most important thing is to keep going and capture the overall shape of the music. It is far better to play a few wrong notes than to keep stopping or going back to correct errors.

BELOW: The Treble clef

Clefs

Music notation for guitar (particularly classical guitar) can be written on a staff of five lines. Each line, and each space between the lines, represents a different note. The pitch of each line and space is

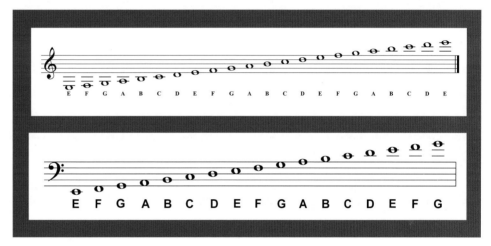

ABOVE: The Bass clef

determined by the use of the treble clef (also known as the G clef) that is written at the very start of each line of music. Temporary extra lines, known as leger lines, are used for any notes that are either too high or too low to fit on the staff.

Bass Clef

For the lower notes required by bass guitarists the bass clef (also known as the F clef) is used.

Accidentals

A sharp sign (♯) can be placed before a note to raise its pitch by a semitone (the equivalent of one fret higher). A flat sign (♭) can be placed before a note to lower its pitch by a semitone. Any sharps or flats will apply to all notes of the same pitch within the bar. A natural sign (♮) on the same line or space cancels the previous sharp or flat.

Key Signatures

The key of a piece of music determines its overall tonality and the main notes that will be included. In music notation the key of any piece of music can be identified by the 'key signature' that appears at the beginning of every line of music. Each major key has its own unique key signature, which consists of a collection of sharps or flats written in a set order; these sharps and flats match those that occur in the major scale for that key. Using a key signature makes music easier to read as any sharps and flats from the key can be written just once at the start of each line and will then apply to all those notes throughout the piece, rather than having to write a sharp or flat sign every time such a note occurs.

The key of C major is unusual in that no sharps or flats occur in the keyscale, and therefore the key signature is blank.

BELOW: C major/A minor key signature contains no sharps or flats.

Minor Keys

Minor keys share key signatures with their relative major keys (i.e. major keys that have a keynote three semitones higher than the minor key). You can tell whether a piece of music is in the major or minor key either by the chords that accompany the music or by the start or end notes. Music in minor keys may also include 'accidental' notes taken from the melodic or harmonic minor scale.

ABOVE: This tune is in the key of C major.
Notice the start and end chords and notes.

ABOVE: This tune is in the key of A minor.
Notice the appearance of the G# note taken
from the A harmonic minor scale.

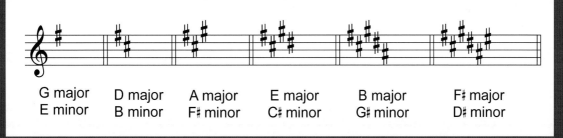

ABOVE: Sharp key signatures.

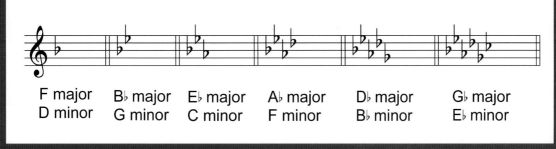

ABOVE: Flat key signatures.

Time Signatures

A time signature is a sign placed after the clef at the beginning of a piece of music to indicate its metre. Time signatures usually consist of two numbers, an upper one and a lower one. The upper number refers to the number of beats in each bar while the lower one indicates the value of each beat. Thus a signature of $\frac{4}{4}$ means that there are four beats to every bar and each beat is worth a crotchet (or quarter note). Likewise, a signature of $\frac{6}{8}$ means there are six beats to every bar and the beats are worth a quaver (or eighth note), and $\frac{3}{2}$ means there are three beats to every bar and each beat is a minim (or half note).

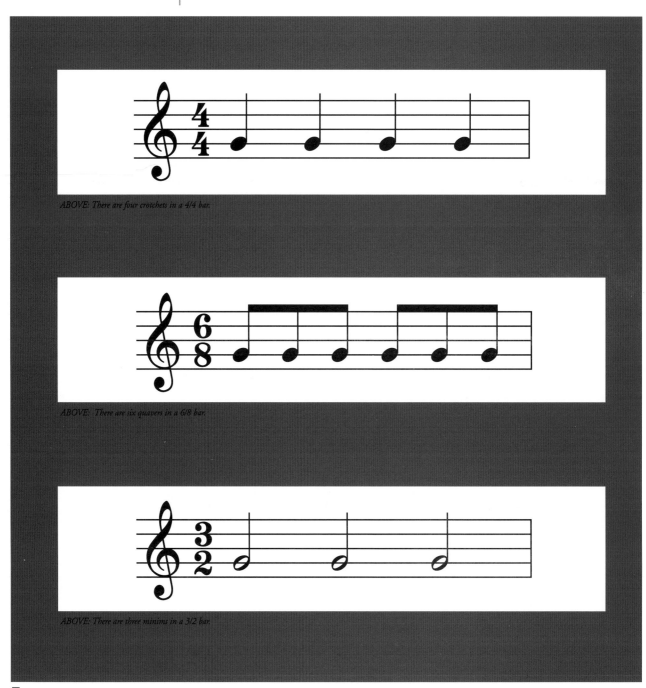

ABOVE: There are four crotchets in a 4/4 bar.

ABOVE: There are six quavers in a 6/8 bar.

ABOVE: There are three minims in a 3/2 bar.

Rhythms And Timing

It is important that a guitarist can recognise the time signature of a piece of music, as this is one of the most important factors in establishing its feel and groove. The most common time signatures in popular music are:

4/4   used in most pop and rock songs

3/4   used mainly for ballads and country music

12/8   often used in blues and jazz

Learning to keep time and maintain an even pulse in these time signatures is a basic prerequisite for becoming a good guitarist. Playing along with a drum machine, or even a metronome, can prove really helpful in developing these skills.

Bar/Bar-Line

A bar-line is a vertical line drawn through a music staff or guitar tablature to mark off metric units. Each bar in a piece of music is the same length unless there are time signature changes within the piece. Many bands use a count-in of one bar when they play a song live to make sure they all start together. Bars in written music notation are usually numbered so that musicians can easily find a specific phrase or passage in the music they are playing.

BELOW: Four bars of music.

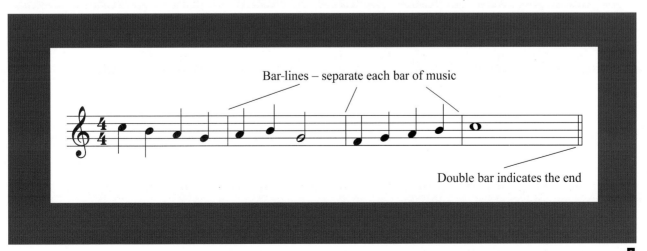

Note Values

The rhythm of a piece of music is written down by using notes and rests. The type of note used tells you how many beats a note or chord lasts for, whilst the type of rest used tells you how many beats a silence lasts for. The diagram below shows the names of the most common types of notes, the symbols for them, and how many of each type of note can occur in a single bar in $\frac{4}{4}$ time. Notice that two or more quavers or semiquavers may be written beamed together.

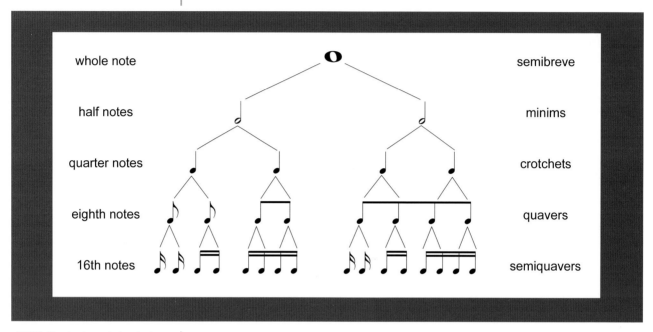

ABOVE: Note that the terminology that is widely used in North America (and increasingly amongst pop, rock and jazz musicians in the UK and elsewhere) is different to that traditionally used by classical musicians in the UK and other parts of the world. In the diagram the modern names are shown on the left and the traditional names are shown on the right.

Rests

The table below shows the names of the most common types of rests, the symbols for them, their note equivalents and the duration of each type of rest in $\frac{4}{4}$ time.

Name	Rest symbol	Note Equivalent	Duration in $\frac{4}{4}$ time
semibreve rest (whole rest)	▬	𝅝	4 beats
minim rest (half rest)	▬	𝅗𝅥	2 beats
crotchet rest (quarter rest)	𝄽	𝅘𝅥	1 beat
quaver rest (eighth rest)	𝄾	𝅘𝅥𝅮	½ a beat
semiquaver rest (16th rest)	𝄿	𝅘𝅥𝅯	¼ of a beat

Dotted Notes

A dot after a note or rest means that the note or rest lasts for half as long again. The chart below shows the values of dotted notes and dotted rests in $\frac{4}{4}$ time.

Name	Note	Rest	Duration in $\frac{4}{4}$ time
Dotted minim (Dotted half note)			3 beats
Dotted crotchet (Dotted quarter note)			1½ beats
Dotted quaver (Dotted eighth note)			¾ beat

Ties

A tie is used to join together two notes of the same pitch, to increase the duration of the note.

In the example right, the C note would be held for the equivalent of five eighth notes. It is not possible to use a dot after the initial C as this would have increased the duration of the note to the equivalent of six eighth notes.

Another common instance where ties are used is across bar lines, to enable a note to last beyond the end of a bar.

In the example right, a tie has to be used so that the C note at the end of bar one can sound for three beats.

Ties can be used to join any number of notes of the same pitch. In this example, the C note is only sounded once but lasts for 12 beats.

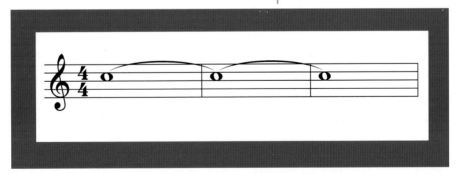

Triplets

A triplet sign indicates where three notes should be played in the space of two notes of the same value.

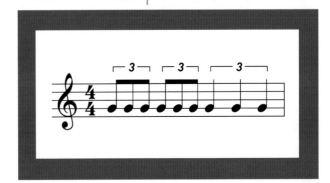

Tablature

Music for electric guitarists is often written in tablature (TAB) rather than standard music notation. TAB uses six lines to represent the six strings of the guitar, with the top line representing the high E string and the bottom line representing the low E string. The numbers written on the lines indicate which fret to play at. A zero indicates that the string is played open.

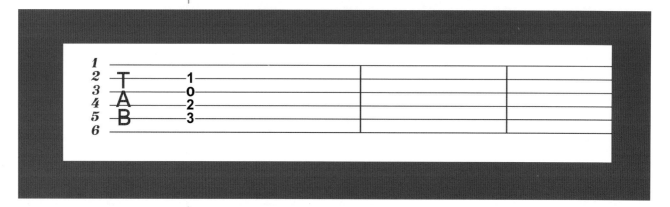

The simplicity of TAB makes it an ideal method of quickly finding the fret positions of music that you have either heard before or can access a recording of, however as it does not normally include any rhythm indications you will not be able to use TAB to accurately play music that you haven't heard before.

Chord Charts

Chord charts are the most commonly used method of notating a chord progression. The time signature is written at the beginning and then each bar is indicated by a vertical line, with two lines to indicate the end of the piece. Chords are indicated by chord symbols. The exact rhythm style that is played is left up to the discretion of the performer, who should take cues from the tempo, style and mood of the song.

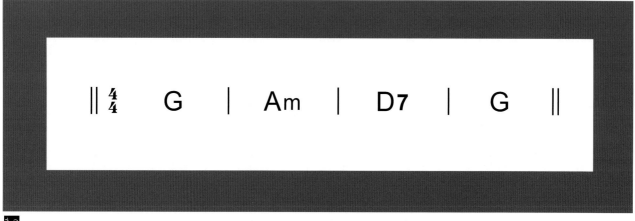

Where two or more chords occur within a single bar the division is shown by either a dot or a diagonal line after each chord to indicate another beat. If no such signs occur then the bar can be assumed to be evenly divided between the chords that appear within it.

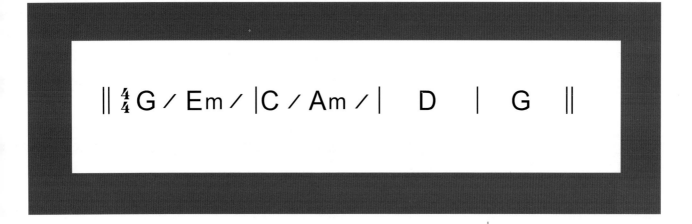

Sometimes chord charts can be quite detailed and elaborate and may even include a fully notated rhythm, as well as instructions about dynamics and repeats. This type of chord chart is quite common for guitarists playing in session, theatre and show-band settings. For general use a more common compromise is for chord charts to contain notated rhythms only at the beginning to set the groove of the song, with further rhythm notation only being used where specific rhythmic accents or features occur.

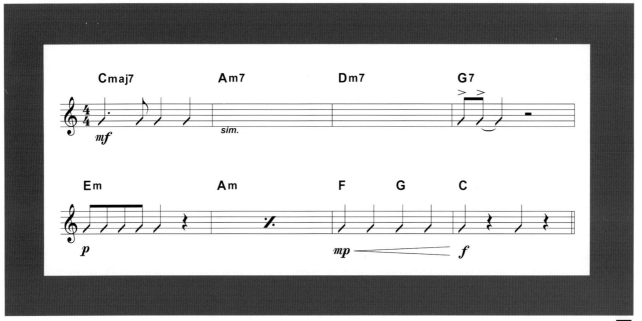

Pitch

Nearly all classical guitarists read music, but if as an electric guitarist you feel that such skills are less important it is still essential, perhaps even more so, to develop a full and instantly accessible knowledge of the location of all the notes on the fingerboard. Having a secure knowledge of which notes occur on which frets is a prerequisite for advanced improvising, as well as providing a secure foundation for chord playing across all areas of the fretboard. Rather than attempting to learn all the notes on the fretboard in one go, it is better to focus on studying a section at a time. Fortunately, the make-up of the guitar fretboard allows it to be naturally analysed in distinct fingerboard positions (often known as 'box shapes'). The most useful of these fingerboards positions are shown below.

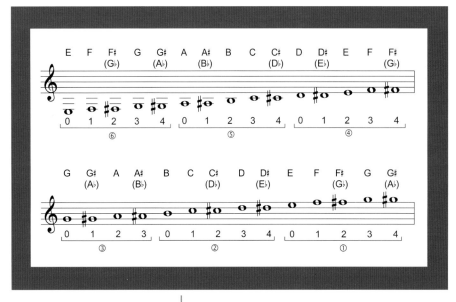

Open Position

The diagram on the left shows all the notes that can be played in 'open position' – i.e. ranging from the open string to no higher than the fourth fret on each string. The numbers in circles refer to the string numbers, whilst the smaller numbers refer to the fret at which the note occurs. The note names are shown above the notation; whether the sharp or flat spelling of a note is used depends upon the key – i.e. whether it is a sharp or flat key (see 'Key Signatures' page 6).

Fifth Position

The diagram on the left shows all the notes that can be played in 'fifth position' – i.e. starting from the fifth fret and ranging no higher than the eighth fret on each string.

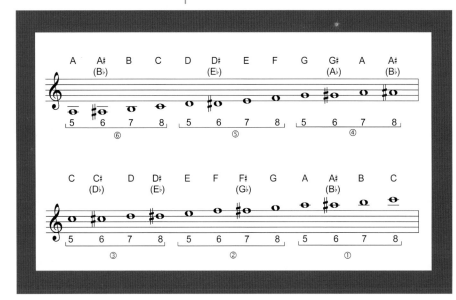

Ninth Position

The diagram on the right shows all the notes that can be played in 'ninth position' – i.e. starting from the ninth fret and ranging no higher than the twelfth fret on each string.

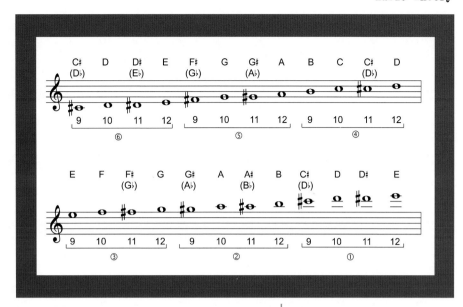

Voicing

You may notice that, apart from the very low or high notes, most notes on the guitar can be played at exactly the same pitch in a number of different fingerboard positions. Although the pitch will remain the same, each note will have a slightly different tone or 'voice' depending upon the thickness of the string on which it is played. For example, the E note of the open high E string can also be played at the fifth fret on the B string, the ninth fret on the G string, the fourteenth fret on the D string or even the nineteenth fret on the A string.

When reading a piece of music, or improvising a solo, it is important to think ahead and choose the optimum fingerboard position so as to avoid unnecessary and awkward fretboard leaps.

BELOW: This E note can be played at the same pitch on five different strings.

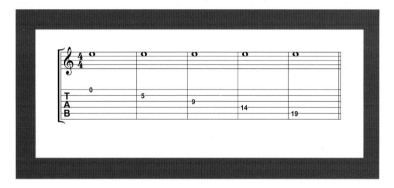

BELOW: Because it includes very low notes, this phrase is best suited to open position playing.

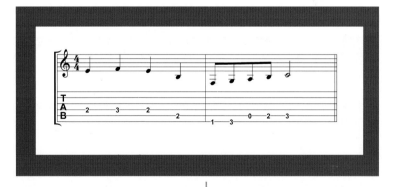

BELOW: Because it includes high notes, this phrase is best suited to ninth position playing.

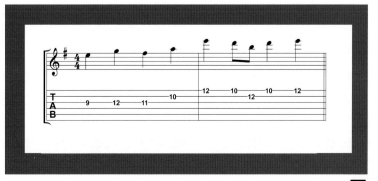

Rhythm

When most people begin learning to read music it is usually not the pitches of notes that prove difficult to read – after a while the note names and their fingerboard location become familiar – rather it is the rhythms (i.e. the combination of note values) that seem problematic. At first it appears as though there may be an infinite number of possible note value combinations, in reality however 90 per cent of music relies on common rhythm patterns. Once you learn these thoroughly, and you can spot a bar or two of a familiar rhythmic pattern, it makes reading music easier. In fact once you recognise the most common rhythm patterns you'll find that any other rhythms tend to be merely variations of the patterns you already know.

Students have a tendency to count just one beat of rhythm at a time. In fact, just as with written language, where a reader looks for the word rather than considering individually each letter that makes up that word, it is far better to try and recognise short but complete rhythmic phrases. This is the method that all good sight readers, such as orchestral players and session musicians, use.

Reading Rhythm

Start with a simple four-beats-per-bar rhythm to establish a steady pulse, and then try some variations on this rhythm by adding eighth notes. Repeat each of the following exercises until you know them from memory.

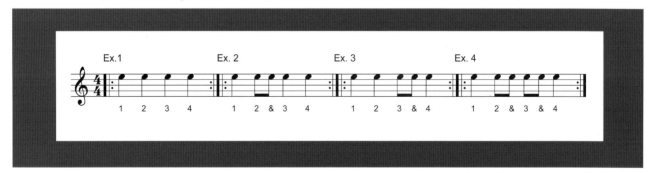

It is a good idea to try and memorise rhythms that carry on across the barline, as very few melodic phrases are contained within just one bar.

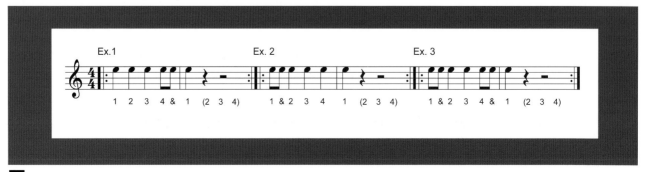

Dotted notes seem complicated to count at first, but once you learn to recognise the main dotted note rhythmic patterns you will realise that a dotted note always has the same effect, i.e. to lengthen the basic note and add a certain lilt to the

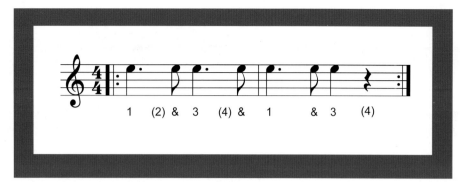

music. For example, when dotted quarter notes are followed by eighth notes this gives the effect of 'long-short-long-short'.

Silences within music are as important to the rhythm as the notes that you play, therefore make sure that you observe any rests that occur in the music.

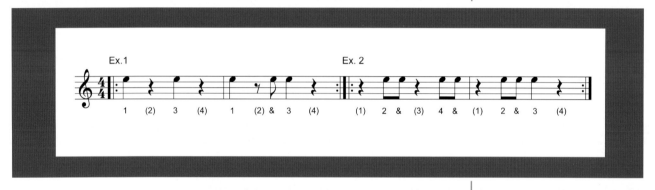

Ties have the effect of lengthening notes, so ensure that the tied note is held on for its full value.

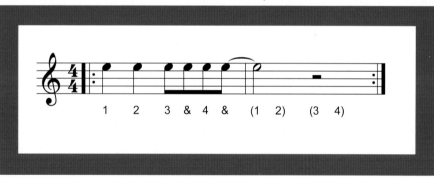

Although it is a good idea to start by learning rhythms in $\frac{4}{4}$ time, music does of course occur in other time signatures. So once you feel confident in reading in $\frac{4}{4}$ time move onto other common time signatures, such as $\frac{3}{4}$ and $\frac{6}{8}$ time.

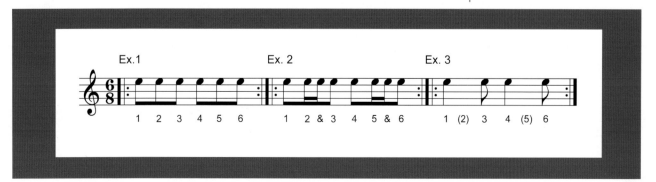

Types of Rhythm

Each style of music has its own core rhythm pattern which helps give it a unique identity. Some examples of these are given below for a range of popular music styles. Of course, this doesn't imply that only these rhythms are used – there are many possible variations and exceptions – but these core rhythms are a common feature of many songs in each particular musical style.

Pop

The ⊓ symbol below a note indicates a downstrum, and the ∨ symbol indicates an upstrum. This combination of down and up strumming gives a light flowing feel to the music.

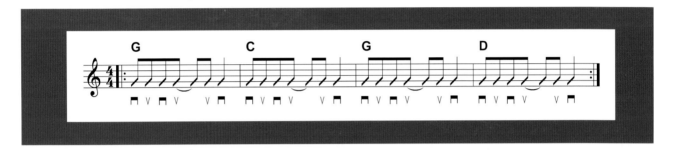

Rock

Using fifth power chords and only striking the bass strings with all downstrums immediately gives a hard-edged rock sound. For an even heavier rock sound, mute the strings slightly by pressing against them lightly with the strumming hand and use a distortion pedal or some overdrive on your amp.

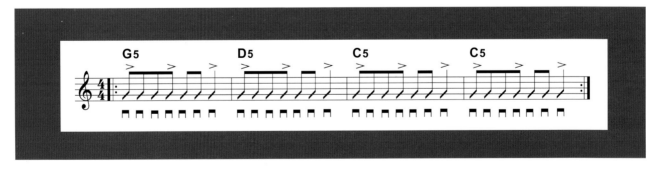

ABOVE: Accent the notes that are marked with the > symbol

Blues

Blues songs, particularly slow blues, are usually played in $\frac{12}{8}$ time rather than straight $\frac{4}{4}$ time, so converting any chord progression into $\frac{12}{8}$ will instantly give it a bluesy feel – especially if dominant seventh or ninth chords are used rather than standard major chords.

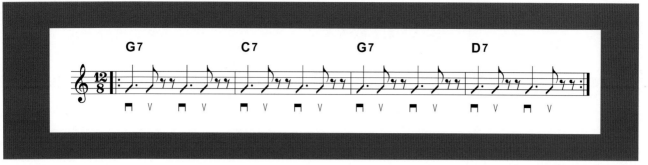

Country

Whilst many country songs are in $\frac{4}{4}$ time, it is one of the few styles of popular music to also use $\frac{3}{4}$ time quite often – particularly in country ballads.

ABOVE: To get a real bluesy feel try playing just the bass note of each chord on beats 1 and 3, and only top strings of each chord with an upstroke on beats 2 and 4.

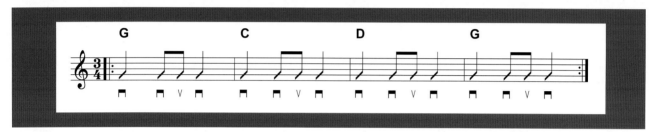

Reggae

Reggae relies on offbeat strumming to establish its distinctive sense of rhythm, and normally only the top three or four strings are strummed in order to achieve a crisp, staccato sound.

ABOVE: For a traditional country style, play only the bass note of each chord on beat 1 – strumming the rest of the strings on the remaining beats

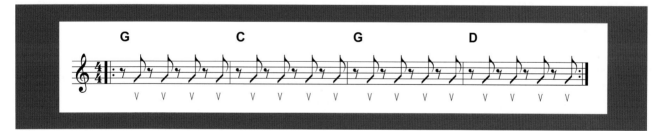

Funk

Funk rhythm playing normally contains short and busy, but crisply played, rhythm patterns, often using only the top three or four strings from each chord. A light and relaxed strumming action is required so that the musical result is rhythmically tight.

ABOVE: Play on the offbeat maintaining a steady, even beat. Strum just the top 4 strings using all downstrokes; reggae players call this 'the drop'.

BELOW: Notice how the basic major chords have been extended into sevenths – a common feature of this style.

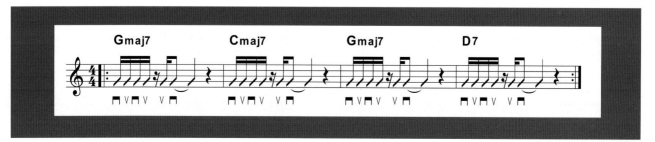

Tempo

The term 'tempo' refers to how slow or fast a piece of music is played. For it to sound as the composer intended, it is crucial to play each piece of music at the appropriate tempo. In classical music the tempo indication is often given in words (usually Italian), whereas in pop music a metronome marking is usually written. The most common tempos are shown below.

Italian term	Meaning	Approximate speed
Largo	very slow	40 – 60 b.p.m.
Adagio	slow	60 – 76 b.p.m.
Andante	walking pace	76 – 100 b.p.m.
Moderato	moderate tempo	100 – 120 b.p.m.
Allegro	fast	120 – 160 b.p.m.
Presto	very quick	160 – 200 b.p.m.

Metronome Markings

The metronome marking tells you the number of beats per minute (b.p.m.) that the music should be played at. For example, the top left box tells you to play at 60 b.p.m.

Metronome markings are normally shown with a quarter-note beat, however sometimes other note values are used. For example see the box on the left.

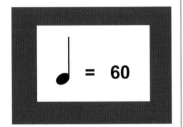

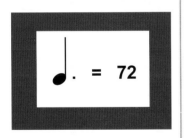

ABOVE: This marking could be used in $\frac{6}{8}$ or $\frac{12}{8}$ time and shows that there should be 72 dotted quarter-note beats per minute.

Timing

Being able to keep time with a regular, stable tempo is an essential skill for all musicians. Novice players can all too easily fall into the trap of unwittingly slowing down at difficult sections in a piece of music, and unnecessarily speeding up during easy or exciting sections. The best way to overcome this is to practice regularly with a metronome or drum machine. Always practice a piece at the speed at which you can manage the most technically difficult section – this avoids the situation of starting at too fast tempo and then having to slow down midway.

Dynamics

A piece of music that was played at exactly the same volume throughout could become boring to listen to, whereas contrasts between soft and loud sections can really help to bring out the mood and musical features of a piece. In pop music these volume changes are often left to the discretion of the performer. In classical music most composers will carefully notate the dynamics (changes in volume) throughout the piece using dynamics markings. The most common of these are shown below:

Symbol	Name	Meaning
pp	pianissimo	very soft
p	piano	soft
mp	mezzo-piano	medium soft
mf	mezzo-forte	medium loud
f	forte	loud
ff	fortissimo	very loud
◁	crescendo	getting louder
▷	diminuendo	getting softer

LEFT: Dynamic markings do not attempt to indicate any precise level of volume, they are only designed to show the contrast between soft and loud sections.

Melody and Harmony

The term 'melody' refers to any series of single notes that vary in pitch and have a recognisable musical shape. In other words the melody is what is commonly known as 'the tune'. Single-line melodies are rarely played just by one guitarist alone as the sound would be rather thin, instead electric guitarists tend to play melodies when accompanied by other instrumentalists, whilst classical guitarists might play melodies in an ensemble with other guitarists. Of course, one of the great features of the guitar is that skilled players can play a melody at the same time as playing a harmonised accompaniment (normally on the lower strings).

BELOW: A short melodic phrase in C major, firstly played as a single-line melody, then as double stops with the melody harmonised a third above, and finally with a harmonisation on lower strings.

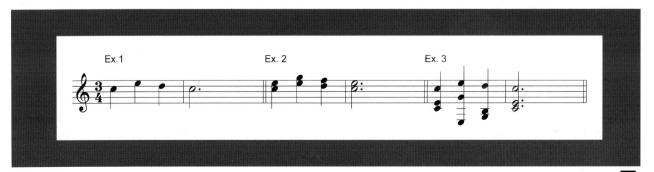

Modulation

Modulation occurs when a piece of music changes key. A composer might include modulation to create musical interest and variety. In pop music this might consist of a simple shift of key – such as the last choruses of a song being repeated a tone higher than the previous chorus. In classical music a piece of music might modulate to any key, although in practice most key changes are restricted to 'related' keys such as the dominant (the key a fifth above the original key), or the relative major or minor key – for example, modulating from C major to A minor or vice versa.

BELOW: This chord progression begins in the key of C major, but modulates to G major in bar 4 and then to the relative minor key of E minor in the last 3 bars.

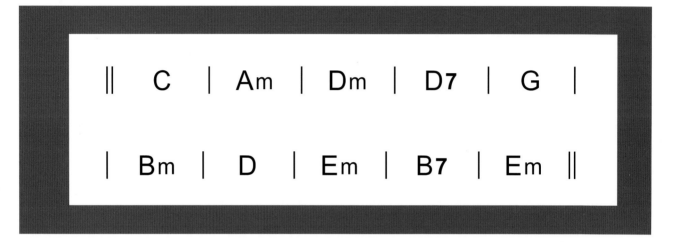

Phrasing

Just as varying numbers of words are combined to make sentences, in music varying numbers of notes are combined to make phrases. Without phrases, music would have no shape or structure and would just be a continuous series of notes. Often it is left up to the player to decide where phrases fall within a piece of music and to interpret the music accordingly, but some composers will include phrase marks above the notation so as to leave no doubt as to what was intended. The phrase marks will help you decide where to leave slight 'breaths' in your playing and how to shape the music. Although it is not always the case, phrases within a piece of music will often be of the same length.

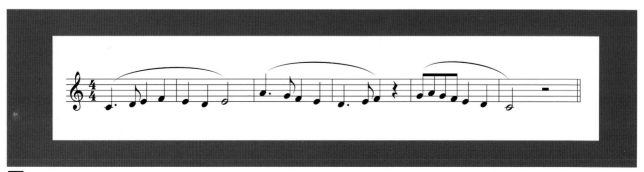

Ornamentation

Ornaments are a method of embellishing a melody by adding notes to it. Ornaments are normally indicated by the use of special symbols. The most common of these are explained below.

Trill

When the letters 'tr' followed by a wavy line appear above a note this indicates that a 'trill' should be played. A trill normally consists of fast slurred alternation between the written note and the note above it in the key. How many alternations you use depends upon the tempo and style of the music.

BELOW: In classical music a trill is often completed by including the note below the original note just before the very end. Bar 2 shows how the trill would be appear if notated in full.

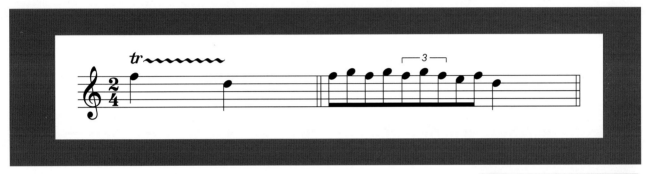

Grace Note

A grace note (also known as an *acciaccatura*) is written as a small-sized note with a line across its stem (see right). Although its interpretation can vary according to period and style, generally a grace note should be played very quickly – crushed in before the beat of the following normal note.

BELOW: A grace note - shown first using its symbol, and then how it would normally appear if written out in full.

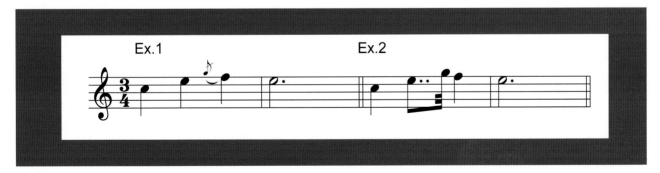

Arpeggiation

An arpeggiation sign is placed before a chord when it is to required to be played with the notes slightly separated, rather than simultaneous. Sometimes an arrowhead is used to indicate the strum direction (see right).

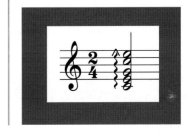

Intervals

An interval is the distance between two notes. Therefore, all melodic phrases are made up of intervals of one kind or another. As many tunes are constructed from the major scale, a good grounding in the intervals of the major scale will help when trying to work out the notes of a melody. The core intervals of the C major scale, for example, are as follows:

C MAJOR SCALE		C to G	perfect fifth
C to D	major second	C to A	major sixth
C to E	major third	C to B	major seventh
C to F	perfect fourth	C to C	octave

The unique sound of each of these intervals can be learnt by either singing through the scale step by step, or by relating each interval to the start of a well-known melody. For example, the Christmas carol 'Away In A Manger' starts with the interval of perfect fourth.

Tone

A tone (or whole tone) is an interval equivalent to two semitones. Two notes on a guitar string separated by two frets are a tone apart. The whole-tone bend (a bend such that a note is made to sound like the note two frets up on the same string) is probably the most common bend used by rock lead guitarists. In the whole-tone scale, each of the notes is a tone away from the next (C, D, E, F♯, G♯, A♯, C in the key of C). Most western music is created out of scales with semitone, tone and tone-and-a-half (a tone plus a semitone) intervals.

Semitone

The smallest interval between two notes on a fretted guitar is called a semitone. Notes on either side of a fret are separated by a semitone. An interval of two semitones is called a tone.

Playing Intervals

Being able to play and recognise intervals on the fingerboard provides a solid foundation for improvising over extended or altered chords.

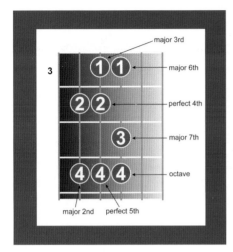

The diagram on the left shows the diatonic intervals of the one octave C major scale.

Having an awareness of minor key intervals will prove useful. The diagram on the right shows the diatonic intervals of the one octave C natural minor scale.

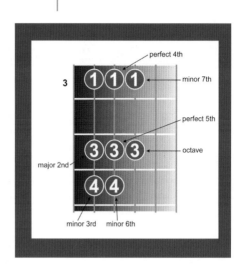

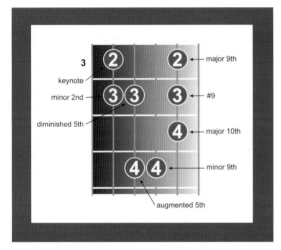

Some intervals occur that are not taken directly from the standard major or minor scales. Here are some of the most useful of these, shown with a keynote of C.

In country and soul music it is common to play licks containing two notes of a fixed interval together. Often, notes from the major scale, a major or minor third or sixth apart, are played as double stops, creating a very sweet melodic sound.

BELOW: C major double-stopped lick using major and minor thirds.

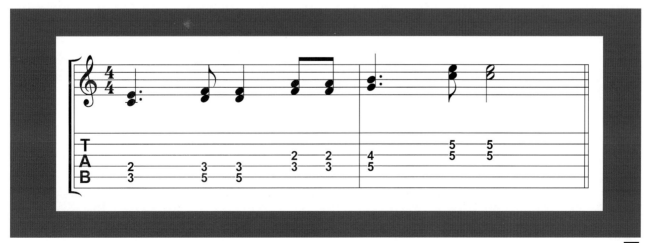

Cadences

Cadences are musical 'punctuation marks' created by using a combination of chords that imply a resting place. A minimum of two chords needs to be used in order to create the resolution. Cadences nearly always appear at the end of songs, however they also occur in other places during the course of a song, such as at the end of a phrase or verse. Recognising the sound of cadences will greatly help you recognise the movement of chords within a progression. A knowledge of cadences is also a great aid to writing effective chord progressions. The most commonly used cadences are described below.

Perfect Cadence

The perfect cadence is formed by movement from the dominant chord (the V chord of the key) to the tonic chord (the I chord of the key). For example, in the key of C major the perfect cadence would be from G (or G7) to C. The perfect cadence creates a strong and complete ending to a phrase.

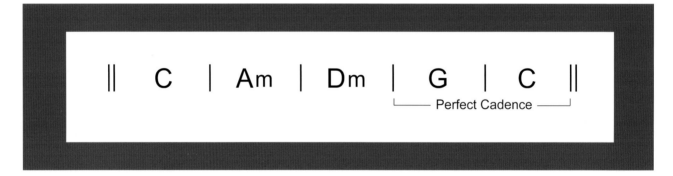

Plagal Cadence

The plagal cadence is formed by movement from the subdominant chord (the IV chord of the key) to the tonic chord. For example, in the key of C major the plagal cadence would be from F to C. The plagal cadence is also often used to end a musical phrase, although its effect is subtler than the perfect cadence.

```
|| C | Dm | Em | F | C ||
                 └── Plagal Cadence ──┘
```

Imperfect Cadence

As the name suggests, this is the opposite of the perfect cadence, it is the movement from the tonic chord to the dominant (I to V). This cadence often serves as a temporary resting place in the music, such as at the end of a verse leading into the chorus of a song.

```
‖   C   |   F   |   C   |   G   ‖
                    └──── Imperfect Cadence ────┘
```

Interrupted Cadence

This is a cadence formed when the dominant (V) chord is followed by a chord other than the tonic chord, usually the minor chord built on the sixth degree of the scale.

```
‖   C   |   F   |   G   |   Am   ‖
                └──── Interrupted Cadence ────┘
```

Minor Key Cadences

Cadences also occur in minor keys. As well as V–I and IV–I cadences, other cadential movements such as ♭VI–I and ♭VII–I are used frequently in many styles of music.

```
Ex. 1
‖   Cm   |   Cm   |   G7   |   Cm   ‖
                      └──── V to I ────┘

Ex. 2
‖   Cm   |   Cm   |   Fm   |   Cm   ‖
                      └──── IV to I ────┘

Ex. 3
‖   Cm   |   Cm   |   A♭   |   Cm   ‖
                      └──── ♭VI to I ────┘

Ex. 4
‖   Cm   |   Cm   |   B♭   |   Cm   ‖
                      └──── ♭VII to I ────┘
```

Repeats

If one bar of music is to be repeated then the symbol on the left can be used. If the phrase to be repeated is longer than one bar, a similar symbol is used but with two slanting lines crossing the same number of bars as in the phrase, and with the number of bars written above it. For example:

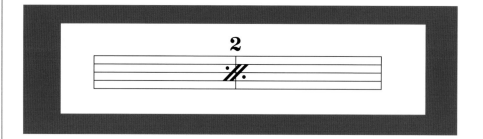

'Repeat marks' are used to indicate that a section of music should be repeated. A double bar-line, followed by two dots on either side of the middle line of the staff indicates the start of the section, and two dots on either side of the middle line of the staff, followed by a double bar-line, indicates the end of the section to be repeated. (If there are no dots at the start of the section, then repeat from the beginning of the piece.) Repeat marks can also be used in chord charts. If the section is to be repeated more than once, the number of times it is to be played is written above the last repeat dots.

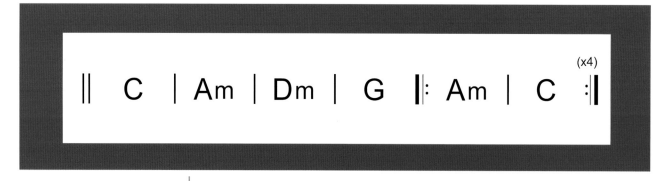

If two sections of music are identical, except for the last bar or bars, repeat marks are used in conjunction with first-time and second-time directions.

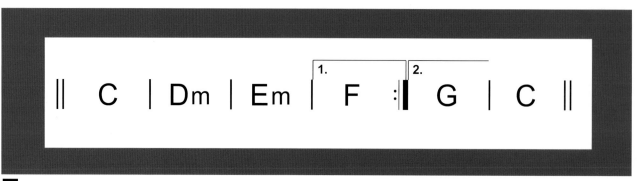

There are other methods of indicating that sections of the music are to be repeated. The most important ones are described below. All have the aim of condensing the information as much as possible whilst retaining clarity and avoiding page turns.

- **D.C.** (an abbreviation of *Da Capo*) means 'from the beginning'. For example, if the entire piece of music is to be repeated, D.C. can be written at the end of the music and this instructs the performer to play it again from the beginning.

- **D.S.** (an abbreviation of *Dal Segno*) means 'from the sign': 𝄋. For example, if the verse and chorus of a song are to be repeated, but not the introduction, D.S. can be written at the end of the music with the sign 𝄋 written at the start of the verse. This instructs the performer to start again from the sign.

- **D.S. al Fine** means 'repeat from the sign' 𝄋 until the word Fine (which means 'end').

- **D.C. al Fine** means repeat from the beginning until the word Fine.

				Fine
‖ Am	| Dm	| E7	| Am	‖

			D.C. al Fine
| Dm	| G	| C	| E7 ‖

• **D.C. al Coda** means repeat from the beginning and then play the coda.

			To Coda ⊕
‖ Am	| Dm	| F	| G |

			D.C. al Coda
| Am	| C	| E	| E7 ‖

⊕ Coda	| Em	| F	| G	| Am ‖

• **D.S. al Coda** means repeat from the sign 𝄋 and then play the coda.

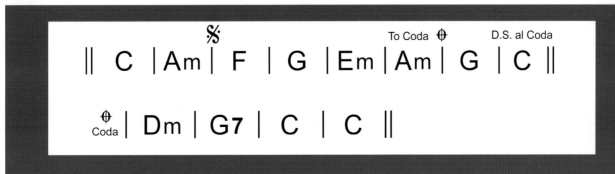

Coda

The term Coda literally means the 'tail' and is the end section of a piece of music. The coda is not part of the standard structure of the song, but is an extra 'add-on' that finishes the song off. It will normally be a variation on a previous section of the music. In popular music it is often referred to as the 'outro'. In some styles of pop music quite often the coda is repeated several times until the song fades out.

In music notation, the start of the coda is indicated by the symbol on the left.

Cadenza

A cadenza is an extended and sometimes improvised section of a concerto that is designed to allow the guitarist the opportunity to display inventiveness, artistry and technical prowess. It is normally unaccompanied and so enables the voice of the guitar to be heard clearly without the orchestra. Although originally intended to be on-the-spot extemporisations invented by the performer, based on the theme of the movement, many cadenzas are either notated by the composer or thoroughly prepared by the performer in advance. The best-known example of a cadenza in a guitar concerto features in Rodrigo's *Concerto Aranjuez*.

BELOW: Some common signs and symbols.

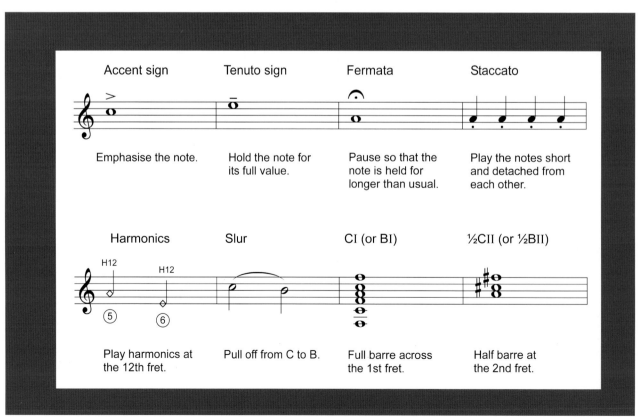

Musical Terms

Here is a glossary of some of the musical terms that commonly appear in classical guitar music.

Accelerando (accel.):	gradually play faster.
Allargando:	getting slower and move to a fuller tone.
A tempo:	revert to normal tempo after a deviation.
Dolce:	play with a sweet tone by picking the strings close to the fingerboard.
Expressivo:	play with expression.
Grazioso:	play gracefully.
Legato:	play smoothly.
Leggiero:	play lightly.
Meno mosso:	less movement, reduce tempo straight away.
Morendo:	allow the volume to die away.
Pesante:	heavy and ponderous.
pima:	picking hand fingers (p = thumb, i = index finger, m = middle finger, a = third finger).
Piu allegro:	quicker.
Piu lento:	slower.
Piu mosso:	with more movement.
Poco a poco:	(make the change) little by little.
Ponticello (ponti):	play by the bridge.
Rallentando (rall.):	gradually play slower.
Ritenuto (rit.):	hold back.
Ritmico:	rhythmically.
Rubato:	vary the length of notes for musical effect.
Simile (sim.):	continue in the same manner.
Sonore:	with a full sonorous tone.
Sotto voce:	in an undertone, very quietly.
Spiritoso:	spirited.
Staccato (stacc.):	play the notes short and detached.
Tacet:	silent, stop playing.
Tempo giusto:	play in strict time.
Tenuto (ten.):	held.
Vib.:	play with vibrato.

BELOW: The modern classical guitar has a tonal range to rival any other classical instrument and is regarded by many exponents as a mini-orcherstra in its own right.

Using It

Transposing

Chords

To transpose a chord progression means to rewrite it changing its original key. The quality of the chords (major, minor, dominant) stays the same, as does their relationship to each other and to the key centre – only the pitch changes. Transposition is a useful skill to have because it means that you can change the key of a song to make it easier to play or to suit your voice if you intend to sing along.

There are two different methods that you can use to transpose chord progressions; both methods will give exactly the same result.

BELOW: John Mc Laughlin is a fine exponent of transposing on-the-fly, while jamming or improvising.

- Identify the key of the original chord progression and work out the chord numbers within the key for each of the chords, then use the chord numbers to work out the chords in the new key. For example, Dm is the second chord in the key of C major; therefore when transposed to the key of D major it will become Em, because Em is the second chord in the key of D major.

- Another way to transpose chord progressions is to change the root note of each chord by the interval of the key change. For example, if you transpose from C major to D major this is an interval of a whole tone. So you then move up all the other chords in the progression by the same interval. For example, Dm would move up a whole tone to become Em.

ABOVE: Paul Simon has experimented over many years by taking old songs and transposing the chords and the melodies to find new combinations and fingerings.

Melodies

The simplest way to transpose a notated melody is to change each note by the required interval. You work this out, by first identifying the original key of the melody, by observing the key signature and any accidentals contained within the melody, then work out what interval is created between the keynote of both keys: this determines the interval that you need to move each note of the melody (either up or down). For example, when transposing from E major down to D major, D is a whole tone below E – so every note of the melody would need to be moved down a whole tone. To confirm that the transposition is correct, check that the 'shape' of the transposed melody follows the shape of the original melody – ensuring that the intervals between each note and the next are the same as in the original melody.

BELOW: The C major melody in the first two bars is transposed up a whole tone to D major.

Reproducing Phrases

The ability to pick up melodies, licks and riffs by ear is an essential skill for guitarists, whether you play electric or acoustic guitar. Traditionally, most electric and acoustic guitar players have learnt largely by this method of listening to recordings and then working out phrases and solos by ear. With the widespread availability in recent years of transcriptions for all styles of music, the emphasis on this approach has changed somewhat, but nevertheless the ability to hear a phrase and then reproduce it on the guitar remains a crucial one. A good level of aural awareness in this area will make learning riffs or songs much easier and quicker than relying upon working things out solely from TAB. Ability in this area will also help with creating solos, as it will enable a direct link between inventing phrases in your mind and being able to execute these ideas on the guitar. Finally, attention should be paid not just to the melodic aspect of aural recognition, but also to hearing rhythms: it is the rhythmic shape of a phrase that gives it its structure.

BELOW TOP: E major – this type of chord has a strong, bright sound.
BELOW BOTTOM: E minor – this type of chord has a soft, mellow sound.
BELOW RIGHT: E dominant 7 – this type of chord has a strident, bluesy sound.
BELOW FAR RIGHT: E diminished 7 – this type of chord has a striking, slightly dissonant sound.

Recognising Chords

Learning to recognise the sound of different types of chords is a very useful skill. Being able to distinguish by ear between major, minor, dominant and diminished chords is helpful not only for working out songs from recordings, but also as an aid to composing your own songs and chord progressions. As a guide, major chords sound bright, minor chords sound mellow, dominant chords have a slightly aggressive bluesy edge, whilst diminished chords sound rather dissonant.

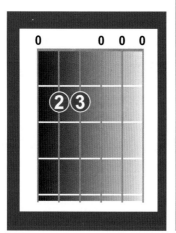

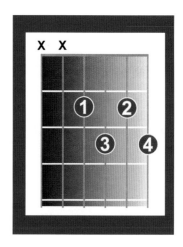

Riff

A short musical phrase that is repeated many times throughout a song. Riffs are typically one, two or four bars in length. Examples of well-known riffs can be heard in 'Satisfaction' by the Rolling Stones, David Bowie's 'Jean Genie' and 'Smoke On The Water' by Deep Purple.

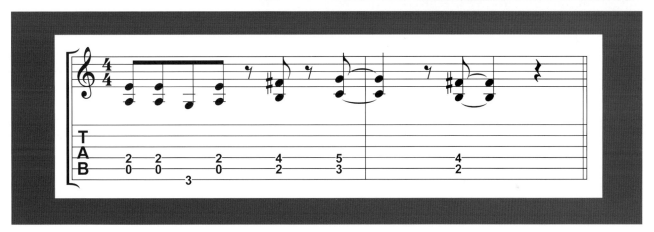

Lick

ABOVE: Example of a typical rock riff – played with fifth power chords. Gary Moore, an inspired rock guitarist, played with Thin Lizzy for a few years, and contributed to their double-guitar riffing style.

A lick is a small musical motif such as a phrase or riff that can be incorporated into a lead guitar solo. All good solo players have a vocabulary of licks which they use in their lead lines.

BELOW: Example of a typical country lick.

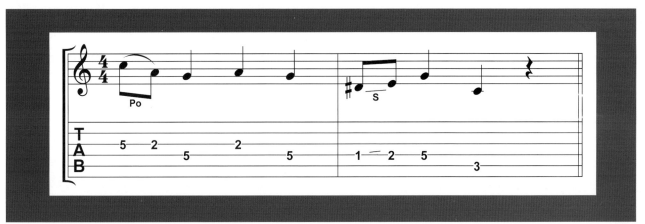

Improvising

Guitar improvisation is often thought of as 'making up a lead solo freely on the spot'. In some senses this is true, but for improvisation to take place there needs to be some structure and foundation behind it. To solo over any chord sequence a scale is required, as this is what defines the choice of notes that will fit with the backing chords. However, not all the notes of the scale need to be played, nor in any particular order (and certainly not in the set order). Once the scale has been learned, the aim is to use it in a melodically inventive and creative way, which ensures that the resulting playing does not sound too scale-like. Short phrases should be used, rather than a continuous flurry of notes and it does not matter if there are gaps. All the notes of the correct scale will fit over all of the backing chords, although some will sound better than others. However, playing the wrong scale over a chord sequence will sound pretty dire: the song's key should be identified before any improvisation begins. Since nearly all songs begin with the tonic (i.e. home key) chord, the easiest method is to check the first chord of the song. For example, if the first chord is A minor, it is pretty certain that the song is in the key of A minor.

$$\| \, {}^{12}_{8} \, C7 \diagup F7 \diagup \; | \; C7 \; | A\flat 7 \diagup G7 \diagup \; | C7 \diagup F7 \; G7 \|$$

ABOVE: C blues progression. Record these chords to practise your lead playing over. Use the C blues scale for your improvising.

Phrasing And Rhythm

The rhythmic aspects of improvisation should be given as much thought as the melodic content: rather than playing the scale in straight time, a far more musical and inventive sound can be achieved by playing some notes quickly whilst allowing others to ring on. Originality is not the main aim of improvisation: it is more often an amalgam of things that have been played before.

A good way to start improvising is to use a well-known melody as a template for rhythm and phrasing. The notes of the melody don't need to be played, instead some of its rhythmic aspects can be borrowed to give the improvisation structure and direction.

By repeating certain series of notes, well-defined phrases will begin to be established, which will give the improvisation structure. Once an acceptable

phrase has been identified, it can be varied slightly when it is played again –
that way it will sound fresh, whilst still giving the listener something
recognizable to latch on to. Leaving some gaps between phrases is a good idea
as it gives the music space to breathe.

Simply playing scales up and down is not enough to make a good solo. Scales
only set the range of notes that will be in tune in any key. It is up to the player to
create melodically and rhythmically interesting phrases from the scale.

$$\| \ \tfrac{4}{4} \quad Cm \ | \quad Fm \ \ | \ A\flat \diagup B\flat \diagup | \quad Cm \ \|$$

Style

The improvisation should fit with the style of the backing: the accompaniment
and the vocal line should be listened to to ensure that the improvisation sounds
right in the context of the song. Improvisation can be practised with other
musicians, or over backing tracks or records, all of which help listening and
playing skills, skills which are key to good improvisation. Lengthy periods of
improvisation practice without any harmonic backing should be avoided, as
it is very difficult to develop a good sense of phrasing and style this way, and
playing can often be become over-busy as it is hard to leave gaps when there is
no accompaniment.

It is important to listen not only to other guitar players but also to the improvisations of other instrumentalists. Their ideas and approaches to phrasing can be adopted, and variations of their musical ideas can be incorporated into future improvisations.

ABOVE: C minor progression. Ask a friend to play this chord progression so that you can practise your lead playing. Use the C natural minor scale for your solo.

BELOW: Eric Clapton is well known for his improvisational skill, seen here jamming with Ronnie Wood (left) and Dennie Lane (right).

Scales

Modes

Modes are scales formed by playing the notes of an existing scale starting from a note other than the original keynote. The most common modes played on the guitar are those of the major scale.

BELOW: C Dorian chord progression. Record these chords as a backing track so that you can practise your lead playing. Use the C Dorian modal scale for your improvising.

|| Cm7 | F7 | Cm7 | F7 | B♭ ╱ Dm╱ | Gm ||

- The **Dorian** mode contains the notes of the major scale starting from its second degree.

|| Cm | D♭ | Cm | D♭ |
| B♭m | Fm ╱ D♭ ╱ | Cm | Cm ||

ABOVE: C Phrygian chord progression. Use the C Phrygian modal scale when improvising over this.

- The **Phrygian** mode contains the notes of the major scale starting from its third degree.

|| Cmaj7 | Bm7 | Cmaj7 | D |
| Cmaj7 | Bm7 | Am7 ╱ Bm7 ╱ | C ||

ABOVE: C Lydian chord progression. Practise your lead playing over these chords using the C Lydian modal scale.

- The **Lydian** mode contains the notes of the major scale starting from its fourth degree.

|| C7 | B♭ | C7 | Dm7 ╱ B♭ ╱ |
| C7 | B♭ | Gm ╱ B♭ ╱ | C ||

ABOVE: C Mixolydian chord progression. Use these chords as a backing track and solo with the C Mixolydian modal scale.

- The **Mixolydian** mode contains the notes of the major scale starting from its fifth degree.

- The **Aeolian** mode contains the notes of the major scale starting from its sixth degree.

- The **Locrian** mode contains the notes of the major scale starting from its seventh degree.

Even though the major scale and its modal scales use the same notes, because they have different keynotes they do not have the same tonality. For example, while the major scale has a major third interval from the root to the third note and a major seventh interval from the root to the seventh note, in contrast, the Dorian modal scale has a flattened third interval from the root to the third note and a flattened seventh interval from the root to the seventh note – making it a type of 'minor' scale.

Using Modes

Modal scales can be used for improvising and for composing melodies. There are two different approaches that can be taken:

- Advanced players sometimes use modal scales as chord scales (using a different mode over each chord). For example, the Dorian modal scale fits over the minor chord built on the second degree of the major scale (e.g. Dm in the key of C major).
- Modes can also be treated as key centres in their own right, i.e. with a 'group' of chords to accompany each modal scale. For example, D Dorian modal scale could be used over a D Dorian minor key centre containing any of the following chords: Dm Em F G Am C.

Box Shape

Most guitarists normally learn scales as box shapes, which show the finger positions for notes in a particular region of the fingerboard. The pentatonic scale, for example, can be played using five box shapes that cover the whole neck, as can the major scale and the natural minor scale. Box shapes are often numbered, with the first finger position starting on the tonic note (first and last note) of the scale. Box-shape soloing is a term that describes solos carried out using a specific box shape or a number of box shapes for a particular scale.

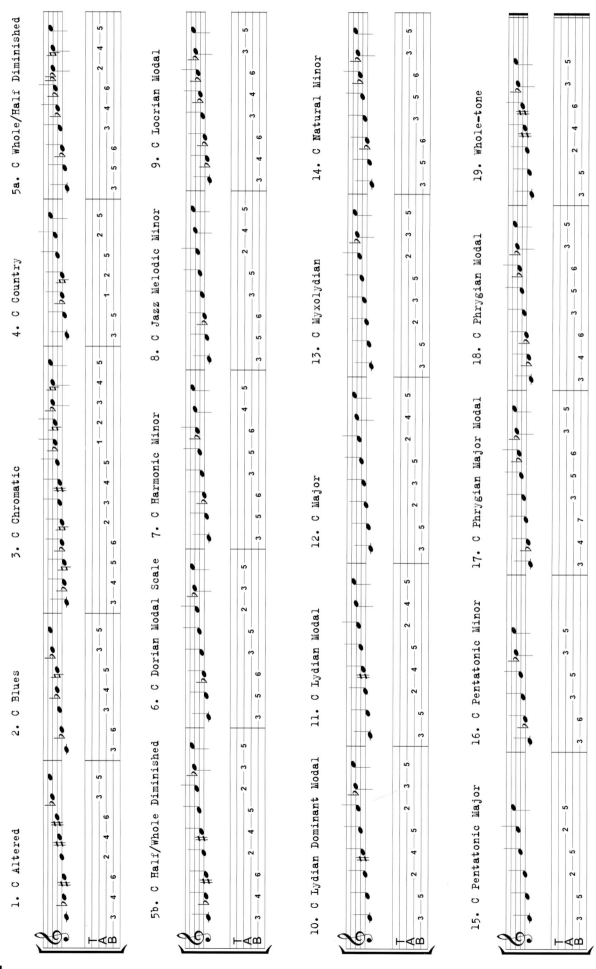

Scale Resource

Altered (see scale 1, p. 40)

The altered scale is built from the seventh degree of the jazz melodic minor scale. For example, B is the seventh note in the scale of C jazz melodic minor, so the altered scale that is generated from this scale is the B altered scale. The B note becomes the keynote of the altered scale, and the remaining notes in the C jazz melodic minor scale make up the rest of the B altered scale.

The altered scale is widely used in jazz for improvising over altered dominant seventh chords (e.g. 7#11, 7#5, 7♭9, 7#9).

The interval spelling:

1 ♭2 #2 3#4 #5♭7 8

Blues (see scale 2)

The blues scale forms the foundation of all blues guitar improvisation. The scale is similar to the pentatonic minor scale, but with the addition of a ♭5 note. It is this note that gives the blues scale its distinctive blues flavour.

The C blues scale contains the notes C, E♭, F, G♭, G and B♭.

The interval spelling:

1 ♭3 4 ♭5 5 ♭7

Chromatic (see scale 3)

This is a 12-note scale that contains every semitone between the starting note and the octave. Because chromatic scales contain all 12 consecutive semitones they do not relate specifically to any particular key. When improvising, notes from the chromatic scale can be chosen to introduce notes that are not in the key of the backing. Adding these 'outside' notes as chromatic passing notes within a solo can make it less predictable and create a feeling of musical tension.

Country (see scale 4)

This is a variation of the pentatonic major scale, but includes the minor third as well as the major third. It is often used in new country and country-rock.

41

Diminished (see scales 5 a&b)

Diminished scales (also known as octatonic scales) contain eight different notes and are made up of alternating whole-tone and semitone intervals. Diminished scales can start with either a whole tone or a semitone.

Diminished scales that start with a whole tone are described as whole/half diminished scales. These are generally used to improvise over diminished seventh chords.

The interval spelling:
1 ♭3 4 ♭5 ♭6 ♭♭7 7 8

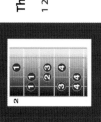

Diminished scales that start with a semitone are described as half/whole diminished scales. These are widely used in jazz and fusion to create a sense of musical tension and colour when improvising over dominant seventh chords.

The interval spelling:
1 ♭2 ♯2 3 ♯4 5 6 ♭7 8

Dorian Modal (see scale 6)

Dorian modal scales are minor scales that have a brighter, less melancholic sound than natural minor scales, which makes them suitable for use in jazz and soul music. Dorian modal scales are created by playing the notes of the major scale starting from the second degree. For example, the notes of the B♭ major scale are B♭ C D E♭ F G A B♭. The second note in the B♭ major scale is C, so the C Dorian modal scale contains the notes C D E♭ F G A B♭ C.

The interval spelling:
1 2 ♭3 4 5 6 ♭7 8

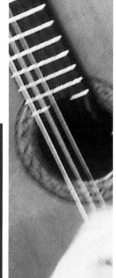

Enigmatic (see scale below)

Although this is a scale with an underlying major tonality, as its name suggests, it has a somewhat unusual sound that can lend a mysterious air to a piece of music. Compared to the standard major scale it is constructed by flattening the second note and raising the fourth, fifth and sixth notes by a semitone. When improvising, the scale can work well over altered major chords, such as major 7♯5 or major 7♯11.

The interval spelling:
1 ♭2 3 ♯4 ♯5 ♯6 7 8

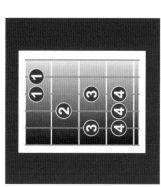

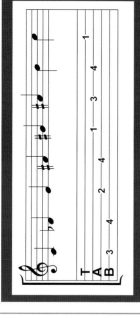

42

Harmonic Minor (see scale 7)

The harmonic minor scale contains the same notes as the natural minor scale except that, in the harmonic minor scale, the note on the seventh degree is raised a semitone. This results in a large interval (of three semitones) between the sixth and seventh degrees of the scale, giving the scale a very distinctive and exotic sound. The harmonic minor scale is often used for improvising in minor keys when the V chord is played as a dominant seventh.

The interval spelling:
1 2 ♭3 4 5 ♭6 7 8

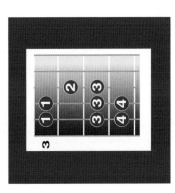

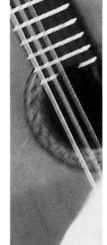

Ionian Modal (see scale below)

The Ionian Modal scale is also known as the major scale. All other standard modes (Dorian, Phrygian, Lydian, Mixolydian, Aeolian and Locrian) are formed by taking the exact notes of the Ionian Mode starting from a note other than the original keynote. For example, the C Ionian Modal scale contains the notes C D E F G A B C, whilst the same series of notes starting from D (D E F G A B C D) forms the D Dorian modal scale.

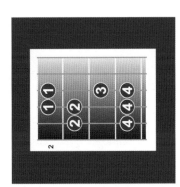

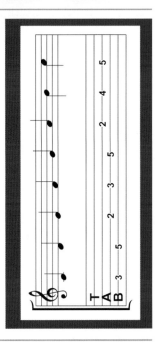

Jazz Melodic Minor (see scale 8)

The jazz melodic minor scale is constructed by taking the natural minor scale and raising the sixth and seventh degrees by a semitone. This gives it a much brighter, almost major tonality that is well suited to some forms of jazz music. It is known as the 'jazz' melodic minor to distinguish it from the traditional 'classical' melodic minor scale which is rarely used in popular music (and which uses the notes of the natural minor scale when descending).

The interval spelling:
1 2 ♭3 4 5 6 7 8

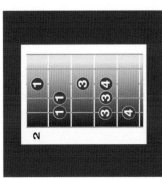

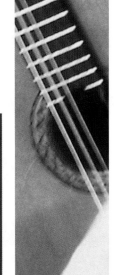

Locrian Modal (see scale 9)

The Locrian modal scale is the mode that starts on the seventh degree of the major scale. For example, C is the seventh note in the scale of D♭ major, so the C Locrian modal scale which is generated from the D♭ major scale is the C Locrian modal scale. The C note becomes the keynote of the Locrian modal scale, and the remaining notes in the D♭ major scale make up the rest of the C Locrian modal scale.

The Locrian modal scale is a minor scale with a diminished tonality, making it well suited to improvising over half-diminished chords.

The interval spelling:

1 ♭2 ♭3 4 ♭5 ♭6 ♭7 8

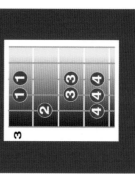

Lydian Dominant Modal (see scale 10)

This is a variant of the Lydian modal scale, but containing a ♭7 interval. For this reason, the Lydian dominant scale is also known as the Lydian ♭7 modal scale. The scale can also be considered as a mode starting from the fourth degree of the jazz melodic minor scale.

The interval spelling:

1 2 3 #4 5 6 ♭7 8

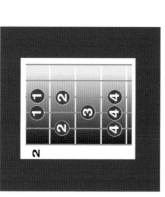

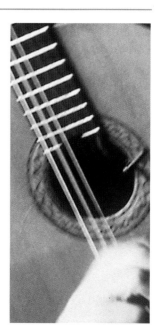

Lydian Modal (see scale 11)

The Lydian modal scale is created by playing the notes of the major scale starting from the fourth degree. For example, the notes of the G major scale are G A B C D E F♯ G. The fourth note in the G major scale is C, so the Lydian modal scale that is generated from the G major scale is the C Lydian modal scale which contains the notes C D E F♯ G A B C.

When compared to the tonic major (the major scale with the same starting note), the only difference is the inclusion of the #4 note in the Lydian modal scale. The Lydian modal scale is often used in jazz, fusion and soul music.

The interval spelling:

1 2 3 #4 5 6 7 8

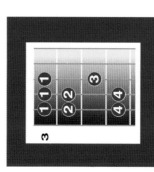

Major (see scale 12)

The major scale is one of the most important scales in music as all other scales and all chords are normally analysed in relation to it. The major scale has a very bright and melodic sound and is used as the basis for the majority of popular melodies.

Major scales are constructed using a combination of tones (T) and semitones (S) in the following pattern: T T S T T T S. The C major scale, for example, is constructed in the following way:

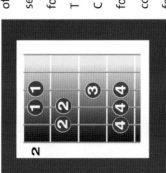

C	to the 2nd note	(D)	=	whole tone
D	to the 3rd note	(E)	=	whole tone
E	to the 4th note	(F)	=	semitone
F	to the 5th note	(G)	=	whole tone
G	to the 6th note	(A)	=	whole tone
A	to the 7th note	(B)	=	whole tone
B	to the octave	(C)	=	semitone

Melodic Minor (see scale below)

This scale is unusual in that its construction varies depending on whether it is being played ascending or descending: when played descending it has exactly the same notes as the natural minor scale, however when played ascending the sixth and seventh degrees are raised a semitone. Use of the scale is quite common in classical guitar music, but electric guitarists tend to use either the natural minor or jazz melodic minor scale instead.

The interval spelling:

1 2 ♭3 4 5 6 7 8
(ascending – left)

1 2 ♭3 4 5 ♭6 ♭7 8
(descending – right).

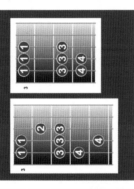

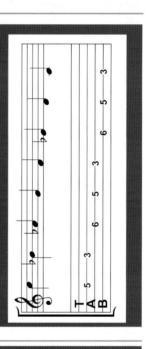

BELOW: C Melodic minor scale descending

Mixolydian Modal (see scale 13)

The Mixolydian modal scale is created by taking the notes of the major scale starting from the fifth degree. For example, the notes of the F major scale are F G A B♭ C D E F. The fifth note in the F major scale is C, so the Mixolydian modal scale that is generated from the F major scale is the C Mixolydian modal scale which contains the notes C D E F G A B♭ C.

When compared to the tonic major (the major scale with the same starting note), the only difference is the inclusion of the ♭7 note in the Mixolydian modal scale. Consequently, the Mixolydian modal scale has a much more bluesy sound than the standard major scale; it is widely used in blues and rock music.

The interval spelling:

1 2 3 4 5 6 ♭7 8

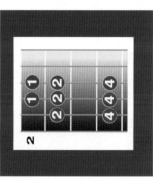

Neapolitan Major (see scale below)

The unusual sound of this scale stems from its mixture of major and minor tonality. The latter section of the scale is exactly the same as a standard major scale, yet it begins with minor second and minor third intervals. It can be used to improvise over minor chords, particularly minor #7 and minor 6. The scale differs from the Neapolitan minor scale in that it includes a major 6th note.

The interval spelling:

1 ♭2 ♭3 4 5 6 7 8

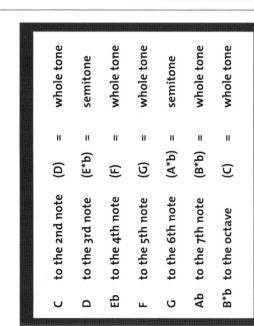

Neapolitan Minor (see scale below)

This slightly exotic sounding scale serves as an interesting alternative to the standard minor scales. The use of the flattened second is important in establishing its 'Neapolitan' tonality. It can be used to improvise over minor chords, particularly minor #7 or minor ♭9. The scale can be easily learned if it is viewed as the harmonic minor scale with the second note flattened by a semitone.

The interval spelling:

1 ♭2 ♭3 4 5 ♭6 7 8

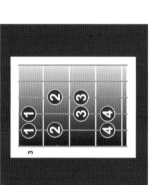
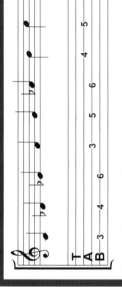

Natural Minor (see scale 14)

The natural minor scale has a very soulful and melodic sound and is widely used in rock and blues-based music. Natural minor scales are constructed using a combination of tones (T) and semitones (S) in the following pattern: T S T T S T T.

The interval spelling:

1 2 ♭3 4 5 ♭6 ♭7 8

The C natural minor scale is constructed as follows:

C	to the 2nd note	(D)	=	whole tone
D	to the 3rd note	(E*b)	=	semitone
Eb	to the 4th note	(F)	=	whole tone
F	to the 5th note	(G)	=	whole tone
G	to the 6th note	(A*b)	=	semitone
Ab	to the 7th note	(B*b)	=	whole tone
B*b	to the octave	(C)	=	whole tone

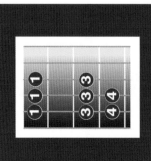
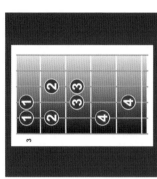
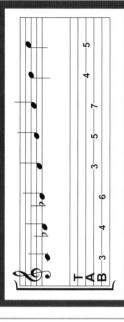

46

Pentatonic Major (see scale 15)

The pentatonic major scale is a five-note scale, made up of the first, second, third, fifth and sixth notes of the major scale with the same keynote. It is a very useful scale for improvising in major keys: as it contains fewer notes than the standard major scale there is less chance of any of the notes clashing with the accompanying chords. The pentatonic major scale is widely used in country, blues and rock music.

Pentatonic Minor (see scale 16)

The pentatonic minor scale is a five-note scale, made up of the first, third, fourth, fifth and seventh notes of the natural minor scale with the same keynote. It is a very useful scale for improvising in minor keys: as it contains fewer notes than the standard natural minor scale there is less chance of any of the notes clashing with the accompanying chords. The pentatonic minor scale is the most widely used scale for improvising in rock music.

The interval spelling:

1 ♭3 4 5 ♭7 8

Phrygian Major Modal (see scale 17)

The Phrygian major modal scale is the mode that starts on the fifth degree of the harmonic minor scale. In practice, it can be considered as a variation of the Phrygian modal scale, but with a major (rather than flattened) third. It is most commonly used in flamenco and heavy metal music.

The interval spelling:

1 ♭2 3 4 5 ♭6 ♭7 8

Phrygian Modal (see scale 18)

The Phrygian modal scale is created by taking the notes of the major scale starting from the third degree. For example, the notes of the A♭ major scale are A♭ B♭ C D♭ E♭ F G. The third note in the A♭ major scale is C, so the Phrygian modal scale that is generated from the A♭ major scale is the C Phrygian modal scale, which contains the notes

C D♭ E♭ F G A♭ B♭ C.

The Phrygian modal scale is quite unusual in that it starts with a semitone interval between the first two degrees. This gives it a Spanish sound; it is widely used in flamenco and heavy metal music.

The interval spelling:

1 ♭2 ♭3 4 5 ♭6 ♭7 8

Whole-tone (see scale 19)

Whole-tone scales are constructed using only whole steps. Between any note and its octave there are six whole steps, therefore the whole-tone scale contains six different notes. Whole-tone scales are rarely used as key scales, but instead tend to be used for improvising over dominant altered chords (such as 7♯5).

The interval spelling:

1 2 3 ♯4 ♯5 ♭7 8

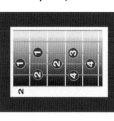

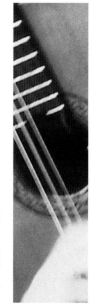

Index